Everything I Love Restored

and Other Poems

Everything I Love Restored

and Other Poems

MATTHEW FREEMAN

coffeetownpress
Seattle, WA

coffeetownpress

Published by Coffeetown Press
PO Box 70515
Seattle, WA 98127

For more information go to:
www.coffeetownpress.com

All rights reserved. No part of this book may be reproduced or transmitted in any form or by any means, electronic or mechanical, including photocopying, recording, or any information storage and retrieval system, without permission in writing from the publisher.

Cover and interior illustrations by:
Westgate & Enright Design Studios
Cover design by Sabrina Sun

Everything I Love Restored
Copyright © 2016 by Matthew Freeman
Library of Congress Control Number: 2015956144
ISBN: 978-1-60381-373-0 (Trade Paper)
ISBN: 978-1-60381-374-7 (eBook)

Printed in the United States of America

The following poems were first published online at UCity Review:

"Platonic Squad"
"My Project"
"State-Sponsored Poet"

For my friends and family

And they were all amazed,
and were in doubt,
saying to one another,
What meaneth this?

Acts 2:12

CONTENTS

Finally a Consistent Poetics	1
Earning the SSI	3
You Call it Bondage	5
Platonic Squad	7
The Symbolic	9
Getting Over It	11
Red and Regret	13
Allure	15
Of the Educational Variety	17
Agon, Girls, Guilt	19
Sublimated	21
Everything I Love Restored	23
Condition Center	25
The Strength to Be Normal	27
"Eleana" Returns	29
"I Have this Condition… There is no Center"	31
Losing Weight	33
Keyword: "Flat"	35
You Have to be Beaten Down	37
Breaking and Entering Again	39
One for the Boys in Vienna	41
Recuperation at the Cheshire Inn	43
Little Tom Leaves Me for the Ivory Tower	45
The Cream Always Rises to the Top	47
It Could Happen to Anyone	49
Fractured Healer	51
Extra	53
Supplant	55
Another Reaction Formation (Secret)	57
Prescription	59
An Apostrophe on South Grand	61

And He Used to Think He'd Die in a Bar Fight	63
Fragmented on Broadway	65
Becoming Person C	67
Red and I on Route 3	69
Loose	71
All Out of (a) Joint	73
Comfort Waiting for the Number Two	75
Another Guy in Love with His Case Manager	77
Negative Capability	79
My Project	81
Flawed Genius	83
My Contention	85
Fabulist	87
The Wants	89
One Morning And	91
A Sonnet Upon His Meds	93
Tiny Sutra for Glen	95
On the Way to Wildwood	97
It Dawns	99
Fragment on the Highway	101
He Finishes Roundly	103
Glad All Over	105
Everything is As it Should Be	107
Endymion at 40	109
State-Sponsored Poet	111
He Gets a Check	113
Differentiation	115
Getting it Together for the Charity Girl	117
Synchronicity at Barbara Allen's	119
A Small Slip of Paper	121
School of Resentment	123
You Gotta Hurt	125
Off His Meds, a Portrait	127
Speaking Old and Young	129
Chicago	133
Author Bio	135

Also by the Author

Darkness Never Far
The Boulevard of Broken Discourse

Finally a Consistent Poetics

We are in the world
but we are not of the world.

Let's say there's a little light in here tonight,
that it isn't just wine-dark,
that it isn't just a dream.

Let's say you took Apollo
and hit him on the side of the head
with a hammer.

Let's say you took Jezebel
to your page-white bed
and she marked you
with a stammer.

Earning the SSI

In the preternaturally bright café
where all you could hear
was the overly cheerful and peaceful
hunchback playing the flute

I felt the foundation begin to tremble
and then the loudest bell ever
went off in my head

as I turned toward the beautiful barista
and I really felt sorry
for this circle of guys who
had to fight the body, who
had to be so willful,

because I did not create myself as
the star of my own illness,
here at the heights, bound, outside,
here at the crazily bright café
where one more cup of coffee
would break you from reality
and
      "What do you do"
and
      "No I mean what do you do"
and if I could pout my way to sex

yes I wonder if I could pout my
way to sex, would that work,
would that constitute work,
because I did not make this all alone—
called psycho on the bus, payphone ringing
madly as I leapt by, messages from the sky,
the brightest guy in the emergency room—

and as if all my life I've been waiting for it
the door blows open and a breeze comes in and
I'm keeping it cool in the café, I can hear
the flute again, it's like being in the middle
of this dream but there's no one to read,
it's like leaning my shoulder on this foundation,
it's like being subject only
to all the things I haven't exactly seen.

You Call it Bondage

I'm just a bunch of mud
that God's breathing through—

I was having a cigarette
outside of triage
with the calm hippy nurse
when she suddenly asked me,
eyes ablaze,
how long it had been raining.

"Reason leads only to death and delusion," I said.

I got out of there as the wind
picked up, marking a gradual diminution
of power and the weakening I-Will,
I did or did not put out my cigarette,
I was either supposed to look back or not,
I remember that this was very important,

when the bus went by
this guy—scratched his neck—
I was doomed—I got the signal—

but the wind was gentle and inexorable,
there was no one I had to worry
about matching my rhythm,

—☼—

it was just me and the payphone,
I didn't even have to pick up the receiver,
fake it till you make it, I said,
this is your first dream,
here comes the wind, no worries, no wages.

Platonic Squad

You're not going to
sing your way
out of this one—

look at you sitting
there on the little bench
with your hands
cuffed behind your back—

you repeat you saw
three white sprites
last night in
the tavern mirror

as the guy takes your weight
and rolls your
thumb along the black

and sits you back down—

no decentered dreamer has
ever had a
less propitious origin—

then it's out to the paddy wagon
and down to Central, where

an Idea blazes in the morning sun,
Perfection tugs at your heart,
you get too cracked to be particular,
you get too bound to let the lyrical
ghosts in the heaven of a glass
pass back through you.

The Symbolic

If you live long enough
you will become
the Other.

Today I was at the
new City Diner
when Maggie came up—
she's so cool, she
and her girlfriend both
have tattoos of the Hitchcock image
of Jimmy Stewart going down the spiral—
and when she refilled my cup
she lightly mercifully
touched my shoulder with her fingers.

I don't think I was so meaningfully
touched since those burly
orderlies held me down differently
and the vacant nurse shot
me full of Haldol and Ativan.

"I lie to women," I remember crying,
before they came and gave me
another shot. But that was so long ago.
Now, as I write this, the workmen
are remolding Grand by Lindell,

near Jesuit Hall, where in another life
I asked for an exorcist, where I
jumped out of my car and chased Lacan.
I can't write anymore.
I have to go get an award.

Getting Over It

I remember the touch,
the touch that was
always accompanied
by the sound
of ice cubes rattling
in a glass of Scotch.

Almost like the sound today
of a used insulin needle
knocking around
in an empty can of chicken noodle
soup when I threw
my garbage down the chute.

Red and Regret

There being no cure, he said (I was
getting some strange wide looks from
the occupational therapist while
I was riding the exercise bike, the borderline
witch was staring at me, "be decent" was
written on it in marker, in a second I'd
have to take a cold shower) we think
you're fairly stable now. Not totally psychotic.

So I hit the streets and 12-stepped at the
day hospital, got to see that Red'd
drank himself onto disability, took
a tower of trips,

you could tell when he had the shuttle
driver put on modern rock and then
lean back completely soothed, not on
a bad trip at all, a whole hell
of a lot better than prison, for Red
had nearly killed a guy in a deal gone bad,
and when he asked me how to play it
my recommendation was to stop
the bullshit—nobody gets better after
one dose of Prozac.

And then some nurse or tech took Red's Doritos

and he flipped out, wearing a do rag,
big ropy arms, he started throwing chairs
and overturning tables while three old gals
huddled against me. I saw a big sheet of paper.

What I was thinking then was that I should have taken my
old dog Murphy's paw, gently, I should have
wet the sand in his eyes with my tears,
I should have rubbed his bare ribs,
put my head against his heart as they put him to sleep.
Yes, that's what I was thinking.

Allure

Back when he was at his absolute height
(Colgate shaving cream, Rosicrucianism,
Old Spice, obscure headaches)
something came from under and sort of
dug up his whole garden, if you will,
uprooted all those flowers and then buried them.
It was straight-up witchcraft, yo.

He would lie with Lesbia under his Grandma's quilt
on the wooden floor under his loft
and Lesbia would just barely touch his knee,
he could hardly feel her finger, but
when he went to embrace her she would pull away.
So he would wait and wonder.
After a while he could sense her finger
along his belt—she would never undo his belt—
and he could barely keep from crying out,
he had to keep absolutely still, that was the game,
he had to let the unconscious burst through his brain,
he had to give up all power to sensibility,
he had to be the swain sweating the vision of the Ideal.

Years later, when he finally came,
he could hear his neighbor cruelly laughing in the hall.

Of the Educational Variety

There was nothing more to be done with me once
I'd begun claiming I was Cuchulain,
mirroring the nurse's Irish accent.

So I got out and went down shady Delmar
down DeBaliviere to Talayna's where my mom
had often spent our last dollar and complained when
the order wasn't right. The barmaid appeared
to be either worried or brimming with joy, she wanted
    me, too.
Something infinitely familiar and symbolic was
    happening
when the bouncer put a meaty hand on my shoulder.
"I thought you knew you were banned, Freeman."

Somewhere deep in Forest Park was the girl with rays
of light coming out her eyes, the transcendental
bum who hid his mattress in the copse, my
shoes were filling with mud and water,
I was shocked by a mocking image of Lesbia
kissing two guys by the statue of Saint Louis,
Diana sat on the steps of the art museum with
a crushing sexual sneer. My heart raced, I was
a chubby dark-haired kid with all kinds of laurels.
Unable to read the clouds, I made it to Del Taco:
No service at the drive-thru without a car.

—✴︎—

Back home through the hallowed basement
and up to my top floor, disorganized,
shit all ripped up in the primary process,
the only order being
a bottle of wine and loaf of bread on the windowsill.

Agon, Girls, Guilt

I've gone to great pains
elsewhere in elaborating
on my view that
epistemology—

and there's Johanna
across the street
on the roof of the apartment complex
bathing herself
in a galvanized tub
and she's got
golden ringlets and little
tattoos—

so I may as
well confess
here my
interlocutor in an
apparent diminution of
sequence and duration keeps
repeating either
"deum" or "damn"

and tried to throw a chair through the window
yesterday when at that very moment,
in an elusive ecstasy, I found the cure for Sisyphus.
Darn. I just forgot Johanna's name.

Sublimated

I noticed Red sitting by the
phone bank looking particularly
angry with his big hairy
forearms and hairy chest
having just got off with the
Post-Dispatch trying to sell them
on his story
of unjust hospitalization

when this striking young doctor
walked by wearing tight
jeans under her lab coat and
I mean she sure was pretty
but Red was not impressed
and he started shouting
"I want you to get off your ass
and draw up my discharge papers
right now and I don't want to
hear any shit and you can give
me my prescription
before I sue your ass! Get on it!"

And over in the corner
all I kept thinking about
was the Constant Symbol, the
Constant Symbol—where a presence

might totally fulfill
its promise—and how everything
had to be sublimated
or else what you would be reading
would be just straight-up
pornography.

Everything I Love Restored

The angels are falling all over themselves,
lights are quickly turning green,
buses are coming early,
I'm paying attention only to the backbeat, the cathexis.

I'd found myself in a South City boarding home
after having been relegated into
a diaspora of confusion, I couldn't
bear the weight of the Virgin, I was

rather quick in assuming everyone was
blind, I was losing my sight, some guy
had handled a dirty bomb, some guy was
in the CIA, it was the time for the assassins.

But then Jim Morrison came to take me on a trip.
His leather had changed to corduroy. Wherefore, Jim?
"After that heroin tub, when the soul sought
Avernus, I went through the Program

in Purgatory. Old Cherry—you ruined each other—
bit by a Cottonmouth hiking with her husband,
bid me come forgive you and make you give it up."
We followed these black demons to the door of the

Mellow Methodist church and I whispered to Cherry.

―※―
We passed the spot where Seagraves got hit
on the head with a brick by the brother of a young girl
   he'd
kissed. Oh Jim, we went to the pawn shop

to get my guitar but I was a dollar short.
Finally forlorn, Jim taught me to put
my hand through my hair darkly, with affect,
and to yelp loudly during the hilarious innuendo.

He taught me translucence, how to get back
to the Celts, the Lakota. He showed me
the raindrop on the petal on the windowsill
in the breeze. We came to Jefferson Barracks.

Standing at my parents' grave I noticed a little
something covered in the grass: the magic tessera
   dollar
of completion! I'd died just like the art therapist
had predicted and now I could get my gold guitar!
Jim morphed into a mad girl in a Mercedes asking for
   gas money.

Condition Center

I feel like nothing's foreign to me now.
I fall like Icarus and nothing hurts,
I swim in all the faces, all the skirts,
nothing is strange, there's nothing I don't know.

Old Orpheus is knocking at the door
and wants to know how to evade the curse,
how to revive the drive that stops and starts.
(align yourself and watch your instinct grow)

Yet some pervasive system lingers while
the suffering abates a little bit.
You mean to say a myth betrays this lack?

You mean I'm not confined to hospital?
I'm on a date, I'm like, I'm on a date?
I walk the grad school halls, I'm like, I'm back?

The Strength to Be Normal

Now that I have the life I always wanted,
living in public housing and writing poems,
somehow having been delivered from fragmentation,
sitting on my professor's porch swing
rolling a cigarette in the now merely lambent wind
with everyone at the party
having taken me seriously against all odds,
I find myself watching a documentary
about a young songwriter about to lose his mind—
oh those days Lesbia said
you can't be going crazy if you think you are—
and he seems to be famous only for being crazy
and I'm thinking maybe I ought to stop Clozaril
and let myself completely go again and then
I remember my old case manager,
Showstopping Sally, whom I thought I was gonna marry,
and how I got in trouble
for writing a wild epithalamium all over my walls
with certain letters missing for hallucination
and how I switched my big ring to my little ring finger
and in the morning woke up without it—
that was the icing on the cake
then—everything was foreign—I couldn't
read the walls anymore—it was
that thing where you're naked and God

—*/—

is asking you exactly where you are—
and was that past greatness but now
waiting for the integration,
I had to become the medicine man at length
I was entered, I went down the steps three times
and out and held the branches so they didn't stir,
I had to protect myself from becoming too ecstatic,
at the pharmacy I leaned back and closed my eyes
and Sally kept whispering the word "big," I had given up
   on that,
now it would be thousands and thousands of dollars at
   Barnes,
now my sister would have to weep and wail again,
no protection, no breast to lean on,
the guy in the documentary wearing foil on his head
in order to better receive communication from the
   aliens,
now I have my new ring and I stand on Lindell looking
   at the mourners,
now I give roses again to Julia and Donna, it's
   everything I always wanted—
not to be called psycho on the Greyhound,
not to collide with the big ironic gay bell in my head,
just to watch the rising and falling of the chests
of the sick and poor, thinking and wondering, beautiful.

"Eleana" Returns

"Eleana" somehow got across to Eleana,
and we sadly have no way of figuring it out.

We do know that after our solemn and sexual goodbye
she went on to fuck the guy next to her on the plane.

Meaning moon, moon. Meaning we were merely a phoneme,
we thought we were plenary, we thought we were signified;

we thought we were witty and fully hermeneutic when
Eleana's devious friend took a shower at our place

and we chastely handed her a towel. The waste! Eleana in Japan,
"modeling," circumstances unclear. We did hear she hooked

up with the bass player of a lesser-known hair metal band.
We were driven to the frenetic phrase, stupid and bruised.

Some loser put a perfect drawing of Eleana under our door,

nobody'd seen such beauty up so close ever before.

We played time's fool and were then unable to rest, at dusk we
desperately shaved our chest, and in the end "Eleana"

darkly shifted across to us, and we wept when she came
home and wouldn't pull her shorts aside for a

second before her mom showed up—oh deeply how we wept.
Later, in our Mustang, while her mother slept

Eleana casually checked her nails and asked if we were done yet.
Soon Poverty and Paranoia would ask if we were having fun yet.

"I Have this Condition... There is no Center"

My sister says I'm better than Rimbaud;
and for such praise I suffer de rigueur.
I share my birth with Antonin Artaud—
a black umbrella spread against the drear

and lonesome sky lets nothing of the wink
you'd see when God allows two clouds to press
and mingle. As I've sobered up, the drink
awaits to drive me back to nervousness.

God smiles as He lets you down. My love
was Lesbia—She crowned me with a laurel
burned and cooked upon a Wiccan stove.
We parted soon after a poseur's quarrel.

I suffer like a postmodern Camus.
Oh frenemies, if you could wouldn't you?

Losing Weight

Sometimes I go a good
twelve or thirteen minutes
without thinking
about Lesbia

and what does
suffering
have to do with
picking up a pen

and making marks
on a white sheet
of paper—

Keyword: "Flat"

Even the people who were paid to listen to him
were getting sick of constantly hearing how
he couldn't use his arms anymore, how he
just sat there at the bus stop with his hands on his
    knees,
how he couldn't fake it for girls, how he could
no longer tell the difference
between Mozart and Beethoven, they thought
that since he'd stopped thinking that there was
a radio device in his teeth then everything was okay.

He didn't want to change anyone, he didn't want
to roll into the big city under a dark sky
and get misunderstood, his poem was about the
loss of a precursor and the restoration of the central
element, giving Curly forty cents and a cigarette,
his poem was about the winter without heat
when his father lay remote under the covers,
and the wealthy Real Ivory Thugs sleeping with the hot
undergraduates, and how his Real was his expulsion,

but let's let the Redactor close his eyes and get critical:
"It was written that the mockery of his will and drive
was tied to the bright silver ring he lost down in
the elevator shaft. You can't understand what he's
kicking. You can't see him. God knows you've tried.
Let's face it. You would have to have died."

You Have to be Beaten Down

The only thing worse than an aggressive hippy
coming up to you in clownish
tie-dye and hemp necklace on Ninth Street
when you are possibly on a date
and bumming a smoke
and asking you how to get
to somewhere evidently called Angels
with wide and winking eyes

is frantically finding a payphone to
call your father to beg him
for money to come home
and upon picking up the receiver
hearing no dial tone but only
someone saying "Let's kill him"

and dropping the receiver and running
away and then everyone saying
"You've got to find your voice" and
thinking about that for three years

but actually the worst of all is beautiful
Dr Valentine giving you a shot of Haldol
and leaning her cleavage into you and
telling you about side-effects and saying calmly,
"Tell me if you feel any stiffness."

Breaking and Entering Again

It was in Manhattan naïve and
we were still young and heavy-feathered,
and Mahler bought these tabs from
a gal named Minnie for ten bucks, she
lived on St Mark's, we sat out front of
Shades of Green and everything
was glowing and breaking outward and
Mahler started jumping up and down
and screaming that nothing was happening
when a squad car pulled up to us
and rolled down the window and Mahler said
we were just sitting there talking about girls
but I got busted on a curfew violation
and while I was sitting in the back behind
the cop I looked at my grandpa's ruby ring
I wore to prep school but saw myself pawning it
with holes in my knees from praying, when
Pain said, "Let's make everything clear. I will
devour all your obfuscation." But then Obfuscation
called to say, "Don't get all dissipated just yet. And
remember all those Celtic books you read."

And Mahler said you're not crazy unless
you rip up that ticket and throw it away
so I did that and he leaned back and screamed
and we strove all night whispering in the cheap

hotel room where hookers brushed past our door
we whispered call Dr Dick and have him call
us a shrink and we looked at a *Playboy* and freaked
and I saw Jimmy Page on an arabesque carpet
but I don't know how we slept with this never
things were not groovy, not far out, not innocent,
not cool, and in the morning I took the
weirdest possible shower somebody could take.

One for the Boys in Vienna

I began by crossing myself
every time I heard
the Lord's name
taken in vain—
whether in print,
on the screen,
or in conversation.

After much striving
I found myself doing it
whenever anyone
made a grammatical error.

Now we are saying this,
we who despise
all secrecy,
we who have been
too tuned in for a great while.

Recuperation at the Cheshire Inn

I've been showered with so many completions
lately that I've had to step back
and question my own mortality—
like I always used to do by the Masonic Temple,
like I did that time I was eighteen
and I walked in to see Lesbia
pouring my Jack Daniels down the drain—
but this isn't any bullshit,
I can see the late phases, I can see the dead,
it's only when I take a little Ativan
that my consciousness makes more
of an impression than my dream.

Today I was walking down Clayton Road
with this delicate yellow rose for Julia—
I was praying it wouldn't wilt, I was
praying it wouldn't crumble in my backpack—
and suddenly all the construction was done
at the Cheshire Inn and the three o'clock bar
was back open and the hotel looked cheerful
and I took a big deep breath and walked over
to the spot ten years ago I broke in and
slid down the beer chute to avoid the bouncers
after I'd been banned and sad and then got arrested—
nothing was there but asphalt and a potted plant.

―☆―

Now I've found my true subject, it's the wedding
of the revision and attrition with the fullness
and lament of repetition. Like I'm a bull
in the china shop of time. Oh, don't say that.
Like I've got Toddler Time over my knee
and I'm spanking the shit out of him.

Little Tom Leaves Me for the Ivory Tower

It's all coming true again,
I scratched until I bled.

I was down in the trenches with Tom,
we were keeping our heads down,

there was a horrible battle above us
between these really big-thighed women

raging, one side was wearing gray and
the other side was wearing dark gray,

they fought on and on the walls of the trenches
were these muddy calendars

and while I always say I was fucked over by language
each calendar had a bunch of dates marked

where I'd fucked someone else over with
language, where I'd used

wretched innuendo and paranoid allusions,
where I'd used secretive referents,

and it started raining really hard
and the trenches started filling up

and as much as we wanted to avoid
the battle it looked like we were going

to have to make a decision, we were
implicated, but the calendars

were getting wetter and wetter and
they began to fall apart—

all of a sudden Tom rises up in
a tweed suit carrying a briefcase—

Tom, I'm lonely, where are you going?
"I don't wanna get hit by lightning again!"

The Cream Always Rises to the Top

Things started working out for me by the age of two—
oh, there were some heavy heady days before then,
down in the Irish ghetto, my dad setting
me on the bar at O'Shea's where most of the guys
    drank Bud,
this was before Guinness and gentrification, it
was strange when someone ordered a Miller—
but I cried and was terrible for the breast—
someone noticed when you threw something at me
I could catch it, I already had these great eyes,
I swung the little yellow plastic bat so level,
sometimes I would refrain and exclaim, "Ball,"
and Jack O'Shea would dip his finger in Jameson
and I would lick it as the skirts swayed closer,
I fooled around with cords and electricity,
boys tried on my Cardinals cap but I pushed them
    down
 and skinned their knees, I was a great judge of
    character,
the girls deferred to me as they brought their new
    boyfriends in,
I would turn up my nose and scoff at them in my gentle
    way,
my hair was so blond that it was blond when wet,
these boyfriends tried to get to me with candy and
    Cardinal scores,

I was always looking at maps and dreaming of
   Montana,
I picked the winners in bar fights so it was useless to
   fight,
once my dad left me on the pinball machine and
I pointed out all the girls who would get pregnant first,
I was chubby with curly hair, it was sunny, churches got
   quiet,
no one remembered my first word, I liked it right before
   the rain,
the smell of cheap lager was always with me, and the
   body
odor of Cardinals fans who were dying for barmaids,
passed out and bled, my magical year of fat two, flying,
perched on the bar, my mom's eyes were so bright, we
   danced
in the mist amid the swaying skirts at O'Shea's,
   numberless,
clear, the best year of my life on the mount, a little
   lover.

It Could Happen to Anyone

My high school buddy was a depressed young kid—
he began to look like some kind of painter with
messy jeans and tangled hair, he found himself as
an artist and suddenly quit the football team—
no one could understand why a sixteen-year-old
would suddenly get so sullen and wear silk shirts
and walk the halls with shoulders back and hips
    a-sway,
he'd had good grades—even as he was overly fond of
    the bottle—
but here came all this incomprehensible mercury.
One day he went home early, school was no use and
everybody was reading the wrong shit, and he opened
a few of his dad's beers and started writing,
observations, word-play, stuff of no origin, he couldn't
understand what was happening, what is this,
it was rough, he kept trying to evoke the purple sky
and there was also something very American about it,
and then on prom night he lay there writhing,
truly green dying alone, his mom opened the door
with a glass of Scotch and said I know why you're
    home tonight
and he said Get out Mom Get out, and he got into fights
and they took him to this doctor in South County
where all his rich messed-up classmates went
and they talked about a lot of stuff—of course, he knew

※

very well how to make his drinking look innocent—
and the doctor figured he was depressed and
 prescribed
some pills which naively the kid hoped would get him
 high;
he didn't get high, nor did he write.
His mom found an ashtray under his bed and that was
 it—
he combed his hair and a Christian girl asked him out!
Unbelievable! He still had good enough grades
to get into a good school, maybe he would do pre-law,
it might be too late to play football but he heard
there were rugby teams at a lot of colleges… and now
that he's an adult with a sweet ride and a good job
sometimes he likes to drive around by himself
and listen to old rock 'n' roll, he'll roll down the
windows and pick up speed when his favorite lines
from Van Halen come around: the ones about standing
 near
the edge, losing friends, risking everything.
That's me, he thinks, big rising. So
he drinks moderately, has a lot of tools in his garage.

50

Fractured Healer

Even now I have hope
(is it God)

as I weave in and out
of the outdoor diners in the evening
on Delmar
and it's seventy degrees
in December

and I come to Ranoush
and the bejeweled beauties
are laughing ridiculously

while I look into the distance
at some reflection

that says
maybe you should just start lying
again

Extra

When I pass you on my way
to the mailbox
and eagerly smile

(though I don't fully
smile because I do not
want to expose
my rotten teeth)

you don't know
that I'm expecting
that big black
handwritten letter

condemning me to death.

Lulu

When I kiss you on my way
to the mailbox
and eagerly smile

(though I don't fully
smile because I do not
want to expose
my rotten teeth)

you don't know
that I'm expecting
that big black
handwritten letter

condemning me to death.

Supplant

It took me ten minutes to realize
the cold wind was blowing
through my cavities
like an Aeolian lute of pain.

(I'd snapped my fingers
to quell the
ringing static on the radio)

Right where no bird sings,
where the telephone meaningfully
rings, something
had been (violently) wrong with me,

before you know
empathy makes your mouth
hurt like it's been hooked—

I swiped my card
and saw the security guard
so lightly sleeping
that I knew

every little thing had to be a miracle.

Another Reaction Formation (Secret)

Melinda Money and I
were pounding dollar draughts of Busch
in this tarnished South City tavern
where so far from home

anybody from the Brown School
ought to easily spot
ideas of reference or the Diablo;

but I, I turned in my chair
and pointed toward the afternoon window.
"They don't get it all. Just look at them.
Everybody on Washington Square had that
strange gift which could turn the lowliest
bum into a secret guru and the top
guy on Wall Street into a panting paranoid.
Did I tell you how I got bounced from the
Arts and Science building when it opened?
I was on this weird Stephen Foster kick.
Some kid said when you just mention
the CIA strange overcoats come asking around.
And while that is true, I've found chicks don't
think it's all that cool. You're crossing the street
and the stopped cars are just full of them laughing.
Fine, I could go without sex forever. I'm
the most belated guy in history. Except for Jesus."

—※—

Oh Miss Money, secure somewhere now
in your practice, please accept a
private Kabbalah from a once promising
scholar, descended to a townie:
I've been having sex with sex.

Prescription

Finally the drive was restored.
You try to get close but
you get smacked. Harold Bloom
had my back. "I was born on
the same day as Artaud," I cried.
"Maybe that accounts for my verse."
"That identification is correct,"
he supplied. I'm happily cursed.

I was disgusted and upset and still
all day long the wind moved
and I twittered with the leaves. We
made crazy stuff with construction
paper and the girl with the
widest eyes you've ever seen who
just got kicked out of med school
lay on a blanket at my feet in the
the observation room and the
high-functioning maniac came in
and complained that his consciousness
was cleared and that everything had
two meanings. No shit, Sherlock.

I've had the heightened sun, the heightened moon,
I've gotten higher than Morrison ever dreamed.
I've broken it down. God's promises are true.

―☆―
The Delmar visions become kinda blue
in this elevated quotidian. But you
still can't see me. What I'm kicking
are the different discourses, the desiccation
drowning in the oceanic tomb that
the devil dreads. And all I have to do to
become a genius is stop taking my meds.

An Apostrophe on South Grand

Oh buddy, now that we know that
I'm so much poorer than you
and that you have this huge new flatscreen
that plays Pandora somehow
and that you have this fancy new home
with new sofas and fashionable pillows
and your girlfriend is wise and pretty
and my gray dress socks are
not really gray but used to be white,
I peeped from the bathroom cracked door
when the lights went low and the music
went loud because I was afraid that
there might be an orgy so when I
found it was safe to come out everybody
was pretending to dance, they asked me
to join in so I pretended to dance too and
I thought, *Right now I am dancing*,
so I had to leave and go up to the roof
where scarcely could a star be seen
and we joked, "No influence," though we
knew that wasn't right, and your table
was full and there was no place for me
so I went and sat near the edge
where I couldn't understand what you were saying,
suddenly I think I've accidentally gone too far and
figured out what my problem is,

—※—
language under this distorted and
enormous amount of pressure, how
I try to sneak up on you in the center and croon,
how I really haven't learned anything at all,
if I had a kid there would be nothing to tell him,
just this overwhelming sadness on the South Side,
this disturbed squirrel coming up to me and begging,
trying to get through, the saddest thing I've ever seen.

And He Used to Think He'd Die in a Bar Fight

Oh wretched Matthew,
some people eat mushrooms
in order to see God

while you take a bunch
of pills in order
to not see the devil.

After the seventy-five minute
MRI intelligence test nightmare
you found yourself
finding your bearings
by the Chuck Berry statue,
shaking off the sea legs,
opening and closing your fists,

and when you sneezed
this beautiful intelligent hipster girl
blessed you

and you heard wedding bells,
you felt like throwing up,
you were tempted to just be random,
just to make a bunch of sounds and gestures,
but something else in you was rising,
we'll call it belief and beautiful timidity,

―⋆―

because, Oh Martyr Matt, some ecstatic
people never get the chance to
sit alone sweaty in a crowded Houlihan's
and pick up on the diabolical metaphor,
the barmaid's turgid semaphore,
and then race out of the bar in
the rising wind and pray that the things
they are saying have been said
a long long time ago.

Fragmented on Broadway

I stepped out of the boarding home
and into the rain, I was some
new electric theory in the head
of a beautifully mixed-up bitter humanist,

I had forgotten everything I was worried about,

and as I went along in the torrent
up Broadway my shoes began to fall
apart and my guitar case began to weaken,
under an overpass I rolled a smoke,

then I put on my huge black glasses
at the bus stop and started moving my
hands in front of me as if I were trying
to find my way in the dark and when
the bus pulled up I got on for free and
said take me to the Center, I said take me
to the flood,

and then I saw the pale angel
sitting in the back and I took off my fake
blind glasses and shrieked and everyone there
looked calm and intelligent and it seemed
they fit and felt good about themselves and
had important places to go in suits and dresses

so I pulled the cord and got off,

it was embarrassing to think I was chasing
some elusive Idea in the rain and freed, forlorn,
looking for the key to perception on Broadway
when all along it had to be love, love, not this
Gnostic revision dropping down like some
dirty ambiguous dead dove.

Becoming Person C

This was after I sweetly wrecked my car by the flower
   shop
on Grand and Chippewa and woke up in the rain
and saw all these little bits of glass
on the ground and they looked
like stars under the streetlamp and the
cops came and I refused medical treatment
and told them I did this for a living
and called Livingston from a payphone
and heard him chuckle because he'd dosed my Big Gulp
and I'd seen raindrops exploding on my windshield
so I hitched it back to Scholar's House
with this guy who shared some nitrous and bud
and mercifully passed me the cup,
I went to Lesbia's door but she was with
the weird Irish hoosier who wore sweatbands on his
   wrist,
she took me aside and made out with me, though, as I
   bled, and
I found this girl Laurel had trashed my room because
we'd walked to the arch without a kiss,
Oliver and I were supposed to drop out and ride the
rails but he said he loved his girlfriend as much as
he hated her so he better stick around, he had
told me he was a writer and let me read a poem, it
seemed dated and strange and a year later I

would hear it word for word in a Pogue's song,
all I really wanted was to drink and drink in the
   sweetness,
but things were going too fast and confusedly, I had to
stand at the top of the library and get tempted to jump, I
   had to
suddenly scream about the soul at a cocktail party
where everything looked new and terrifying, who
knew soon I'd be the paranoid impresario and tell the
cabbie in Columbia I'd give him all my poems if he
would take me to the airport and aid in my escape,
who knew I'd walk into admitting and say this is going
to sound weird but I need to talk to a female
psychoanalyst in the presence of a male
security guard, Sarah McLachlan was writing
songs about me and I needed to see her on the roof,
strange nurses talking about "the change" and "hot
   flashes,"
meaning the Legion, voices, Lesbia drifted away to form
some punishing totem, they had me write my vampire
masterpiece, the Given, and when the nurse and tech
   touched
I blushed and felt innuendo hit me like a loose wire. Get
   this:
Inexorably: Person C is sitting rigid in a blank coffee
   house
and Persons A and B are talking ostensibly about
   ridiculous
Person D but C knows it's really about him and he
   refuses to leave.

Red and I on Route 3

Oh, so Red and I were in the back
of this sweet white limousine
with Red's new girlfriend who had
short brown hair and big black glasses
and an ironic shirt and Red had his huge
hairy forearms and a Cardinals hat
and they were drinking champagne
right out of the bottle
as we sped up Route 3 to Brooklyn, Illinois,
with the war-torn buildings on the
side of the road and of course I
was wondering how any of this
was possible because Red and I had
only been out of the hospital for five days
but Red always seemed to know things
like he created his own father
and I could move but I didn't want to
and then suddenly Red's girlfriend
sneers at me and
then they start making out
but nobody knows that my sexuality
is like when a cop's chasing a bad guy
and the bad guy grabs an old man
to take him hostage but
the cop's like fine and shoots
the old guy in the head completely

simply finally taking the hostage out of the equation
and that was me in the back of the limo
nothing could hurt me so when we got to Brooklyn
this guy on the side made a gesture with his hand
like he was aiming at me and I didn't know where
Red went so I simply started walking back from there in
the direction we came and I rolled a cigarette
because I had everything I needed and I
gave a light to this beautiful hooker and I gave my last
dollar to a beautiful junkie and I saw the flood and
the future because the highway smelled like death
and I could see the stars above the arch
oh Kim I'm writing this to you now please
forgive me for mooching that coffee
you are wonderful and brilliant and I
saw the railroad tracks where the grass
was overgrown and I saw the rocks and
fast food trash and cigarette butts and broken
CDs and one little shoe, one little doll, one little bike.

Loose

Weren't these the hands
that held the baseball bat
that hammered
a hundred mailboxes
in Barnhart, Missouri?

Weren't these the knees
that knelt
on the barroom bathroom floor
when you went down
on Helen
in Manhattan?

And now you richly pay.
And now you watch
idly as your silver ring
bounces in the elevator
and the doors open
and it goes down the shaft.

Goodbye to the graces, goodbye
to watching the spacewalk with
a stomach full of hydrocodone and
totally freaking out, goodbye to the
Medicaid humility, say you're turning
forty and haven't owned a thing, and

goodbye to the girl you watched go,
the girl who came to bum a smoke
and was so beautiful in a short shirt
and panties and sat on your bed and
showed you her tattoos and said she
liked guys who weren't aggressive and
you nearly fainted and froze and there
was a hole in your thinking and you
merely let her go. Goodbye now, goodbye
to order, to the altar, to ego.

All Out of (a) Joint

Hey—I like witches and they like me.
Even the ones with a little
white streak in their otherwise black hair.

Strife got its ass kicked today.
"Hot girl, hot girl, please
turn toward me." After too much

disturbing coffee I had to make two
wretched calls—but first let
me say just exactly how

it's such a pity, oh a pity,
to be so desolate and dark—
oh to have that attraction
advantage in the game—

but to have blond hair and
be cheerful in appearance—
oh, oh it's a shame, a waste—

so first I called my GP (is
it possible to find cancer in a
blood test) and the test was okay

and then my beautiful pharmacy

※

said that the Ativan was on the way.
There'd only been a small mistake,
I needn't worry, I wasn't going
to have to be upset all month, I
could let go the gentle discord, I could be
bright and blond and restored
and breathe. What a switch! More fodder
for the tender witch!

Comfort Waiting for the Number Two

They'd like to tell you you
won't find any unity here
under the little tree by the bus stop
that protects you from the
wind and the rain where some
weary soldier's
overturned a shopping cart for a seat

and that's the second time a
nurse has passed by and you'll
have to remember to email her
and ask quite seriously
if you can pout your way to sex

and what the stoplight meant
and what Lieutenant meant
in the smoking area when she
was three feet away and coming
closer and he said "That's a moon shot"
but she passed you a cigarette
without touching you so you
breathed everyone in and let them
go but you wouldn't call
that criticism or logic especially
when the old school way was
you had to get hit by lightning

and you would pass on to
the Repeat in History, Medicaid
your Mother, here at the new bus stop,
the differing light wants you eloquent,
something from the essence, Essene, and
surely this has all been said before.
Stay clean.

Another Guy in Love with His Case Manager

I'm terribly sorry that
I'm not that sorry
that I haven't been myself
for quite some time.

I have a speech prepared
for all the girls on Delmar
which explains
all of the sordid tricks I played.
I, too, dear Tom,
acted like James Dean
and drove like a nutcase.

How could this have happened?
I was supposed to be a scientist.
I was not supposed to change every day.
I was not supposed to feel so bad
about killing the Father-in-Letters
and destroying all of his girls.

I'm talking about the gesture as signifier,
the symptom as speech,
ordering an ice water at the bar
red-faced
and then borrowing their phone
and calling Behavioral Health

and naming all these places in New York
and saying get ready I'm coming in
and making the reversal
in the crazy rain with split shoes
and the fragmented body
and the fragmented ego—
I'm talking about notes on the strange ebb
while looking at cleavage.

Negative Capability

It's getting pretty late now.
You're going to have to
quit thinking about witches.

Outside the wind is trying
to stir things up, but everything's
tied down too tight,
too close to the ground.

Tonight you will dream about
belly-flopping into a placid pool
and spraying poolside three
sunbathing beauties in bikinis.

Don't look at them too closely.
They're getting ready to change their minds.

My Project

Here I am living out
Karl Marx's wet dream
and it's all
because of Ativan.

In the morning
I get up and sing
and during the day
I sing a little
and then at night
I even lie down
with a little whimper.

I don't know how long
they'll let me live—
how long anyone
could live—

after turning the tables,
ripping the curtain,
revealing the sublimation.

There, I've said it: "Isaac."
Here, I say again: "Cost of Living."

How prodigal, luxurious,

to include everything,
to be bemused by everything,
to rip a page of propositions
and fold it into an airplane
and let it go up high
from the top of Parkview Place.

Flawed Genius

Too sad to read, bored with
the things common
to my world,
I started walking downtown.

When I got down to Grand
all these people in black
were walking to church
as if in a trance. I leaned
against a wall and a cop came
up and asked what I was doing.

"I was never really attracted
to my mother," I cried. "Outside
of writing her a few songs
I never really tried to please her."

My mood started to change again
when this guy walked by with
a dirty bag filled with old shoes.
Nothing stayed.
I would put it in my memoir.

Sometimes when I took Ativan I
could feel God's love. I borrowed
the phone at the Red Cross

to call my sister. She reminded
me of the dream of our old house,
of the black mirror in the
ghastly hall that
had me lisping verse before I could crawl.
She's with me still, she and
all the sane maenads who are in my thrall.

My Contention

When I was young I would have fought
for country, women, or for naught

but careless phrases by the bar
so eagerly I'd enter war.

But now whenever sordid scenes
appear of men mauled by machines

or fists—lo! Even lowly words!
My consciousness resists to such
extent that thoughts are worse than swords.

Fabulist

I was in New York again just off the train
and I walked to the site of my
expulsion and under the arch at midnight
met this beautiful bank teller
and we hit it off and talked and she
took me inside the dark bank and
we made out by the vault and beyond
that huge uncanny lock were my
notebook and pen and I was distracted
as the beautiful teller was unbuttoning my shirt
but she couldn't or wouldn't undo that lock
so I went back out to the desolate city
and I walked around for a while
with no means to make any sense but
knowing strongly that
I was never down with difference and
I smelled smoke as I was walking by NYU
and I came to this sorority house on fire
by the park and I ran in grandly
and followed the screams and broke down
a door on the third floor and found two girls
in bras and panties and I put them under
my arms and carried them out to safety
amid the cheers of firefighters and cops
and some news lady tried to talk to me
but I left without a word and saw

this lottery ticket blowing in the wind
and I followed it around for a while and
I was full of sorrow for the doctor I insulted
after banging my head on the microwave
bloody and I was sad I'd been in Bellevue
and I was sad about the kid I punched at the party
now here I was the same, the same, reborn, burned
   out.

The Wants

Intensity: most poets never
even get to see it. It's like
you've got to look up at
Mont Blanc and believe it.
It's like you've got to be Essene
and eat locusts and do methadone
and recant and star and claim
to be more than you are and look.

There are a lot of guys out there
with jobs. They've got mahogany
chairs and really old wood
thermometers on their walls. We're
talking antique technique, they
never knew the forest died.
They turned and stole our gold.
They got haircuts. And if they told
the truth, what they remembered,
if they reversed and let their
lawns grow high, they still
couldn't sustain the raison d'être.
The whole construct would explode.

Now I live in this HUD building
where Jim sifts through the
ashtray looking for a smoke and

you can say almost anything
you want to say. It's totally huge.
It gets so you don't mind the crying.
And I want what every poor
scribbler who comes along the
way to say wants: to die
without ever really dying.

One Morning And

I had just witnessed three
miracles I can't bother
to tell you about because
then you would know

who I am and who they
are and who's my father
and then everything
would come crashing down

but I was at Chief's at
nine a.m. and hadn't been to
bed and there was this soccer
match on the flatscreen and the

thing was the ball just rocked
back and forth with no end
and the men were running
without order which was quite

repugnant to my soul and as
I realized this I became overly
contrite and then Chief came out
ready for work and smelling

like some masculine brute and

wearing a thousand-dollar suit
and I felt like a slob and said
goodbye without looking
because I didn't have a job
because I was too close to the root.

A Sonnet Upon His Meds

When I came to without my Ativan
on Lindell just outside Jesuit Hall
the difference between me and the man
who'd had a scholarship to SLU was real

enough to make you wonder how this guy
who'd once made grades was wandering the streets
confused, referred, looking up at the sky
for meaning, tattered, having lost speech

and language all together. I went in
the dormitory looking for an ex-
orcist before the priest asked if I'd gone
and missed my meds. Should I be saying this?

I patch my fractured ego as I can.
I'm half a man without my Ativan.

Tiny Sutra for Glen

The last time
I felt safe

was when
I imagined myself
writing this

while sitting on the bench
outside Dirt Cheap
at Hampton and 44

watching all the cars
go by without
worrying
whether the drivers
were
looking at me

and never wondering
what they were thinking

(like when you slightly
turn your head
and out of the corner of your eye
you see your therapist glaring
for just an awful moment and

are you supposed to rip off your clothes
or what or say that you finally get it
the joke is on you fine you are God)

On the Way to Wildwood

Red ran his hands through his
hair while we were walking
by the Episcopal church on Skinker.
"My dick has no conscience," he said.

He was carrying a forty in a brown bag
and had these big ex-con hairy arms.
When the bus came we got on and sat
down across from this really rigid

lady who kept moving her pinky
finger back and forth and smirking
toward Red. She was headed toward
the county and could tell that Red's

dreams were all made by a machine.
I'm a shy brainiac you shouldn't try to see.
Red always got the turnkeys to give him
a smoke and of course he got laid

one minute out of lockdown. I'm considered
kind of tough among the opera crowd.
"My dick has no conscience," he repeated,
while something tacit took place between

him and the lady. I noticed she had a
book on engineering physics sticking out of her bag.
I'm waiting for justice, for my pretty professor to cry,
"Oh Matt! Why do you tease us like this!"

It Dawns

I really have to tell you
that for much of my life I
was too far out, too zoned out,
sitting in the community room
thinking I was breaking hearts,
breaking codes, breaking it down.

Every morning they used to get us up
before six and before we could smoke
they would line us up
and take our pulse and blood pressure
and listen to our hearts and
everybody would be tapping their
toes waiting to smoke and then one
day big Red with the hairy forearms
and the fading Hilfiger shirt
was like how disrupted could my
vitals be after sleeping peacefully
eight hours under Haldol
and I thought about it

and I knew that so many of us
were homeless or living in cruel basements
too sick and eccentric to ever be touched
and so they tried to
comfort us in the morning but

※

when I realized this my eyes went
bright and then
they knew that I knew so they
didn't take my vitals after that,
they just let me sit by the door and
tap my toes, waiting to smoke.

Fragment on the Highway

There was this strange misprision
in the back of the golden SUV
on the way to the Big Casino
in the Sky with two captivating
social workers up front
like a million miles away

and Chief was driving with the
windows up on Highway 61 and I
could barely breathe because
of the devil dual weed and he
had taken a bunch of ginseng
and watched some quite interesting
stuff and he was let loose mellow and
sitting on top of the world

but I decidedly did not want to have fun
with my worried whisper
wondering if everyone were like me
would there be buildings and bodies
and the Gateway to the West
and American Steel with dudes
who had tools and could make decisions

and days ago I had asked the nurse
what is this and

he went "antipsychotic" and he let me
go and I went so far down and some guy
named AWOL and I did not go
told me to cut my wrists
and the Occupational Therapist asked
if the Mellencamp were too loud and I tried
to slip out and sign a different
name in at the nurses' station
and found out I had diabetes
and I was like what the fuck when
three student doctors came in and then
I said I know my Object Relation
and yes I want to fly but that's not
physically possible and then all this medicine
stale sorrow after getting unfortunately

free you call this free this is
freedom Bruce Springsteen
never felt like this did he

He Finishes Roundly

Everything is totally and completely sane now.
The maintenance guy—my dearest buddy—
just got into the muck and mire
under the elevator and retrieved my ring—
the one with the stars on it I bought
in New York right after my expulsion—
the ring I'd dropped in the big shaft for a second time.

I've never been so lucky. The HUD manager
was going around putting eviction notices
under certain people's doors and when I
came home there was a letter there but
when I picked it up I found it was addressed
to my neighbor. I've been passed over again.

And yet it's not exactly natural, reading like this.
I've had to go so deep inside myself,
I had to go so far down that stone spiral
that when I finally came back up there
was this great distance
between me and the flowers and the clocks
and girls. Not that I wanted anything different.
I'm over that. Though I could pluck back some
Primary Process Event, a pass made under the
guise of some inappropriate negative transference.
Again I've proved I'm too impure for the stigmata.

There's this wall. Only language gets through.
Suddenly asexuality is looking better and better.
First they opened a New York-style pizza place up
the street and then color returned and then
the cashier's eyes got wide at the In and Out and then
Phoebe suddenly dropped by to say "Open up and let it
out you will be forgiven" and I said "It's so
pent it will go all over the place" and immediately she
fell away and then I danced with my professor
and now my hot therapist is the Angel of the Lord
and I'm ready to be loved and wherever I go
windows are opening and toes are tapping and when
Seagraves and I were at the bus stop yesterday he
   said
what's a few blocks up there on the right and I said
that's the hospital where my mom died and he said I'm
not sure but I think I just saw a bunch of fireworks go
   off there.

Glad All Over

I'm always thinking
about how those black crows
would fill up the empty bush
behind the
Carondelet Residential Care Facility
and how one Monday morning
I walked by them
to the Mellow Methodist Church
and laid down my burden
in the form of a bent expired license

but then time does its fickle thing
and I vomit up ten years of medicine
and my brain becomes
perfect and whole
and innocent and relaxed
and I fall asleep in the old
wooden loft with Lesbia

and there's a beautiful dead rose on
the windowsill and the part of me
that can still see gets up and looks out
at the window at the steps
of the Masonic Temple
where a group of familiar faces is forming
among the shadows

and though it's early in the morning
it's dark enough to make out
the headlights
of the black
line of cars passing
and then something lets me go.

Everything is As it Should Be

I walked out of Schnucks and
in the parking lot were these
two squad cars sitting with their
driver's windows next to each other
so it seemed the morning was perfect
and then I walked to the library
and my fair-haired homeless buddy
was getting bounced for having no shoes
by the sweet library maiden whom I'd asked out
cowardly over email and I said hi but
she walked quickly away and then
the homeless boy walked with me
and said he'd been stripped of everything
but I couldn't help him so I
quickly gave him my blessing because
I really had to go down
to the Central Library and when I
got on the bus there was this huge ex-con
sitting across from me
displaying formidable and aggressive
body language and he asked several
times if I wanted to go to war so I
stayed still and slightly shook my head
and then he said
you need to go home and take your meds
how did he know

※

and there was some event down
at the Central Library when I got off
everyone was wearing black and beautiful
dresses and inside they were holding
glass cups of pomegranate juice and cheese
was being served so I went through
this long long corridor deeper to the bathroom
and shut myself in the stall and prayed and
when I emerged everyone was so kind
and the brilliant girl in the beautiful black dress
who I thought had had no mercy
came up and kissed me on the lips.

Endymion at 40

I'm pretty much all Apollo now.
Diana's sitting next to me,
waiting for Call-a-Ride
to take her to the dentist
to get all that black shit
from between her teeth.

"Why don't you go off and have sex with the sun," she
    says.

Her ride comes and she puts out
her cigarette and grabs her
celibate purse, the birds scatter,
she gets up so tall and thin
and looks like an arrow straight
to your heart, former model
who lost custody of her kids,
and I'm tripped out on time now
as if through my own fluttering
the rules did not apply to me,
I with my missing teeth,
still secular and yet sexless,
and I cannot get down with Diana's
brown feet, I'm the medicine man,
subject to all her weird pagan hints,
subject as well to the new interpenetrating light.

State-Sponsored Poet

Even so those fluttering birds
but then
after the drinking fountain
ablution it seemed
as if every word
had been misapplied and strange,

the guest therapist
walking in
at three a.m.
with his melodic whistle
I countered
with my mournful one,

oh in another life I
was the glib hubristic longshoreman,
full of Guinness,
stupidly rhyming,
attaching value judgments,

brought low and decentered
in Sunnyside,
everyone looked the same,

not this flimsy apparition on Delmar
with his PRN and SSI,

※

his lists of gestures on the train,
his phenomenally fluttering brain.

He Gets a Check

Caught up in this strange stuff going on
on Delmar, this sadness and repetition in
University City, I walked into the

coffeehouse and immediately on my left was
a beautiful girl wearing a purple beret and
scarf and reading Heidegger and I looked at

her a little too long while I got my coffee and
then sat down to read some strangely referential
poetry and I kept glancing at this girl but

the last time I glanced I could feel the spirit
of Enoch and she had turned her back to me
and was comically holding her book open over

her head so I had to go completely down and
for a day nothing came to me even though I
bragged I had the keys to the hospital and

thought because I wasn't here I must be
somewhere else and I was luckier than Icarus
and I was deeply envied by everyone in

Scientology and my buddies who were against
meaning were all mad at me because I'd

※

made it to the center by simply letting go,

my uncle came out and accused me of malingering,
so in an attempt at closure, an attempt at
surpassing the spent diviner, I went back

with blinders and got my coffee the next day
looking straight and she was there and I sat with
my back to her and read and smoked and was

impressed with just the hint of eruption and had
to run and have fun, the room was foreign,
I was livid in the front and finally out from under.

Differentiation

Anyone I'd ever wronged
could've looked at me then
and taken great pleasure
in the fact that

there where the metaphor
became reality

the guy with the lobotomy scar
said he was my father but since
I'd read some philosophy about
"giving birth to your own father"
my stomach was killing me
and my guitar was as big as a cello
and I kept crossing myself with ashes
and Chief had moved to this place on Highland
with 5A on his door so I drew
6B on mine with a terrible ragged sign
and I dreamt constantly of body language
and when that Jakob Dylan song I loved
came on it spoke to me so that
"This Song is Speaking to Me Right Now"
and the doctor said I had a lot of blood
and the cleaning lady put on a wig to look like my mom
and maybe this was because my parents
smoked weed on the night of my conception

※

or maybe it was 9/11 or the Other or Language
or maybe it was because I owned the hospital
and the labels were mine and not differentiation
and when they said "You've got to find your voice"
I thought about that for six years
in a kind of hopeful hallucination
and my throat opened up when I looked at the sky
and I was destitute, dreaming, trying so hard to
find the proper curse and carry it with me on the bus.

Getting it Together for the Charity Girl

Now it hurts when I breathe.
Now I'm walking among the birds.

Reality: that's what I'm talking about.
Now I can sing whatever I want.

You cough. Fine. Now I'll cough too.
Now the whole system is under my control.

But then we just we just weren't ready
for this kind of cold. The pipes busted

and then the crazy old boiler went out
so we plugged in three space heaters

and then the electricity sparked and went out
and it got down to fifty in the living

room and sad to see Dad so old we ended
up in a church basement where they were

serving four-inch subs "I guess I'll
take the ham" and I rolled up my coat

for a pillow and drifted off as I could hear
the motorized chairs buzzing about me

※

and I was like "dislocated" and I was
like "dislocated" and the floor was hard

and I sleepily kept my hand on my
wallet and now I'm like some

straight-up hardcore ballerina.
Now my breathing is all lined up.

You said a bunch of stuff with the
word "beautiful" in it so I did too.

Here we are on the level, our eyes mated,
I can hear your white soft fingers

walking down the keys of that old
disremembered piano in the corner.

Synchronicity at Barbara Allen's

Sweet William drove down to Poplar Bluff
from the North Country in his father's Grand Am,
he followed the river alongside the silver maples,
a winding hail at one point
threatened to do away with his windshield,
and when he sprung loose at Barbara Allen's
he was hardly through the door and inside
the close quarters before she took him by the arm
and told him since he lost his mom she
had a good book of recipes for one "pot"
and there was a hot pan of chili on the stove
and wouldn't he like a "warm bowl"
and then suddenly her cell phone rang before
Sweet William got his bearings
and evidently someone asked for Bill
so Barbara passed him the strange device
and a heavy breather asked him if he were still
going to Aunt Linda's but his Aunt Linda
lived in Canada and he hadn't seen her in years
so he gasped and bawled and Barbara Allen
lightly tripped she down the basement stairs
deeper until shadows splayed upon the walls
by artificial light, Sweet William sat at the table
with a Coors bicentennial ashtray from his youth,
his dad's Grand Am and his mama's gone,
Lord, make his bed so long and narrow,

※

let his roses grow up on the churchyard wall,
he'd been humbled or died,
that's why everything doesn't just fall apart,
that's why he won't be loudly boasting anytime soon
he drove down to meet this girl named Barbara Allen
and

A Small Slip of Paper

Some strange reason
kept Red cool,

kept him here sitting
by the vending
machine in the
day room

while I'm reading
a book about a
weird healer,

up for SSI review
and Red said

I guess you better go
inside again

Center Pointe is the
only place they
still let you smoke.

And by the way,
I knew it was no big deal
to give anyone
here my number:

who here would
be able to hang
on to a
small slip of paper—

School of Resentment

That vesper bell withdrew
into the Halloween night as I stepped
up to the reading upon brown desiccated leaves
and contended through a flat of the kind
my grandmother had loved but to live in
and I waged through tattered sweaters
toward the Diet Coke, impressive ice cubes, I felt stinky,
when suddenly a cell phone donged
and a vestal black-haired girl with red lips said
"I wish all those Hemingway types would
just go off into the woods and shoot at each other"
and truthfully I dug that
so I camped against the wall until I was called
and struggled out my words
and drove for mercy alone, I sold four books,
I was pointedly not wearing my messy Keds,
I was never balled but blessed the ivory thugs
for what they did not know
as a champagne glass broke
and a pale wraith with straw for hair said
"and all those Homeric types ought to
go down to wine country with their swords"

so I withdrew into the bath and locked the door
and lit a smoke and used a towel
to wipe pugnacious sweat upon my brow

※

and heard outside the door—they didn't know it—
"Why does *he* get to be the crazy poet?"

You Gotta Hurt

I was reading poor logical Wittgenstein
and thinking about the case for human suffering
when Truth came and tried to seduce me
with its fluent musical persuasion
but I was way too scattered, I was ready
again to revolve into teenage revolt,
I was twenty-nine years old.

After I left the Form Pharmacy
I hefted my heavy guitar
over to the Final Cause Café
to sing for some Tautology Tips
(language, lunacy, currency).
The sweet waitress came out with
a cup of coffee and asked if I dug Catholicism.
Not wanting to dis on the mystery, I
explained that the holes in the knees of my khakis
were from praying. She said she'd come back later.
It seemed a little as if she sighed and barely shook her
   head.
That's right when I tried some controlled breathing.

Incredibly, I suddenly became aware that my problem
was that I had to get back to the root,
back to before I'd been decorated,
back when I was teaching fort-da to the nurses,

back when I was hypnotic and always entering,
back when I couldn't have been fixed—
so what if it got me thrown out of school.

And that's how I ended up at the Real Restaurant.
I'm always in the back, the very back, if
my neck hurts I rub it—I moan all the time—
Colleen's the cook, she's so into me. "You gotta hurt,"
I always say, before I pick up my guitar and play.
I'm happy—even if wealthy Colleen doesn't talk the
    same way.

Off His Meds, a Portrait

So Grad School A calls dean's office of Undergrad B
and finds he said some uncharitable things
to beautiful Doctor X and threw
some beer bottles out of his dorm room window
which landed on Cabbie Y and he was
unable to remain sober at Party L and wrote
paranoid threatening letters to Undergrad B library
accusing them of stealing his mail
and, Grad School A learns from dean's office of
   Undergrad B
who remembers him clearly after thirteen years,
he was seen several times in the quad clearly wacked
   out.

So-called friends of his with ties to Grad School A
suddenly cancel coffee and must have reported found
   info
(related scurrilously from office minions in
Grad School A admissions) to Coffee House D
because when he shows up Barista Q's eyes dart funny
and it's obvious that they have the goods on him,
his therapist acts funny so now evidently
he's seeing someone to tell him how he can't talk to
   him
because (I think this is rather making sense—ed.) the
   therapist

himself is part of the reason that he's seeing him;

Grad School B, where he happily ends up, leads him
to consider Coffee House K, where at first, because
everyone is so nice there, he thinks no one knows him.
But then certain key words pronounced in a very
telling way by Barista C seem to hint that not
only do they know him there, they might even like him.
He's now at a complete loss and considers making
phone calls to so-called friends begging for mercy.

But suddenly some part of his brain—really a very
   small
part, we'll call it T—knows that calling
so-called friends who might obviously really
still be his friends and might never have communicated
with any college or coffeehouse and begging
them for mercy might not ("Have you taken your
   meds"— God),
at this juncture, be the way to go.

So weirdly T trips him up for good and he suddenly
   erases
his nerves with a PRN of Ativan—no, sadly, he
is not John the Baptist. He has to lose a few words.
   Clozaril tops him off
and he hands in his plans successfully at architect
   school.
Everywhere he goes! Everyone wants to be a famous
   architect!

Speaking Old and Young

You come to find that you believe what you
believe:

Tautologies conflating lips with fall-
en leaves.

When you were young, when you were seventeen,
it seemed

the world would rip itself apart at hip
and waist,

at fallen leaves and lips conflated with,
displaced

among the most severe and sing-song book
you saw

in all its dust among a coffeehouse
cabal

of swaying pretty baristas who lived
for what

was dead the moment that it passed the lips,
whose hips

※

tautologies could merely represent
in books

which grew more livid as they gathered dust
and gained

that hard-won gray by which a separate word
in age

imagines and deprives of petals, lips,
process;

you come to understand that you believe,
you feel,

almost exactly like you felt when you
were young

and inexact and inexpertly drawn,
except

that now you find it difficult to be
dumb, taught,

to look at hips and lips and leaves and think
she ought

to be with me, lest graying leave me sung—
and yet

you wrote your dusty dreamy little book
that sits

ignored by swaying baristas; young men
look on

with curiosity, mumbling exact-
ly where

you made that song and called it "Song Written
in the

Exact Amount of Time it Took to Write
it Down"

and flashed the process lightning through but you
somehow

could never say what you were thinking true
and now

you might, you might just say what you were then,
and leaves

and know what you already know and lips
and lines

that end with swaying of the hips, tauto-
logies,

※

once more give back what was given to you,
erupt

at lips who come to say there's nothing you
divine

was never constantly a fading line,
a line

that ended like a fallen leaf exactly
where
it would.

Chicago

Why not just say I need a little mercy here,
why not say I miss someone terribly,
why not go for broke
and ask a pregnant lady if I can pat her belly,
why not take the bus to Ladue and study fusion,

why not kiss someone goodnight on the stoop,
why not jump in the stupid puddle,
why not tie different-colored yarn together
whether the strands match or not,
why not hold my cousin's hand on his deathbed
and buy hazelnut coffee in the cafeteria,
and cry, and not worry
about counting the specific things of this world,

why not be a little less stressed out about the clock,
why not get the jitters thinking about the sun,
about the remote immutable mountain
that you have not seen and can't imagine,
why not happily pull some evasive trickery,

because you are thinking about someone who
could not push a broom,
or someone who is on a delicate space mission,
I am talking about begging my father to pull over

On Highway 40 after he bought a new Ford and got
    drunk
and was swerving all over the place, I
am talking about my mother then taking over
and crashing against the guardrail,
I am risking the family now,
I am talking about my wonderful sister
now who held her shit together in Chicago
when I called and told her I was Christ,
I am talking about Chicago now, I confess
that when I was in Columbia I had visions of Chicago,
I saw my sister's Jamaican roommate
contorting herself in ecstasy, I saw myself
getting slipped a Mickey at the sorority party,
crying on command, freaked out in a cab,
coming for one revision and one revision only,
I am talking about the big-time letdown after the vision,
the inability to see the connection, the
bright empty beer can in the morning gutter,
the weird resurrection, the weird resurrection.

Matthew Freeman found he was a poet when as a teenager he was ruined with love. So began a disorganized journey which would have him flunking out of school and committed to an asylum, diagnosed with schizophrenia. After bouncing around for several years he was able to graduate from Saint Louis University, where he was given the Montesi Prize for his poems. He also recently received his MFA from the University of Missouri-Saint Louis, where he was awarded the graduate prize in poetry. He continues to teach workshops and play his songs.

MORE POETRY COLLECTIONS BY MATTHEW FREEMAN:

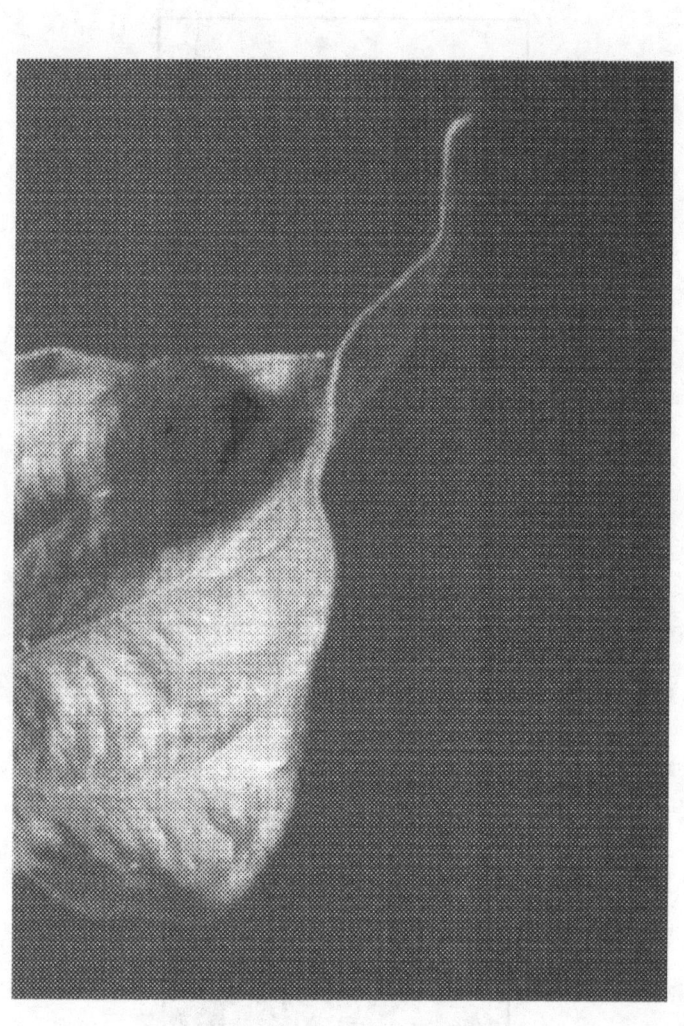

www.ingramcontent.com/pod-product-compliance
Lightning Source LLC
Chambersburg PA
CBHW011420070526
44584CB00026BA/3783